Nita Mehta™

SIMPLY DELICIO

CURRIES

vegetarian

Nita Mehta™

B.Sc. (Home Science), M.Sc. (Food and Nutrition)
Gold Medalist

SNAB
Excellence in Books

Nita Mehta™
SIMPLY DELICIOUS
CURRIES

Snab Publishers Pvt Ltd

Corporate Office
3A/3, Asaf Ali Road, New Delhi 110 002
Phone: +91 11 2325 2948, 2325 0091
E-mail: nitamehta@nitamehta.com
Website: www.nitamehta.com

ISBN 978-81-7869-440-5
Revised Edition 2015

Printed in India at Infinity Advertising Services (P) Ltd, New Delhi

Contributing Writers:
Anurag Mehta
Tanya Mehta
Subhash Mehta

Editors :
Sangeeta
Sunita

Distributed by :
NITA MEHTA BOOKS
3A/3, Asaf Ali Road, New Delhi - 02

Distribution Centre :
D16/1, Okhla Industrial Area, Phase-I,
New Delhi - 110020
Tel.: 26813199, 26813200
E-mail: nitamehta.mehta@gmail.com

Editorial and Marketing office
E-159, Greater Kailash II, New Delhi 110 048

Food Styling and Photography by Snab
Typesetting by National Information Technology Academy
3A/3, Asaf Ali Road, New Delhi 110 002

Recipe Development & Testing:
Nita Mehta Creative Arts - R & D Centre
3A/3, Asaf Ali Road, New Delhi - 110 002

Price: Rs. 125/-

Introduction

To most, curry simply means vegetables with gravy, along with a combination of spices. One always thinks a curry to be something oily, rich and hot. We have tried our best to change this concept by reducing oil and chillies and adding flavourful spices. The curries are flavoured with exotic spices like nutmeg (*jaiphal*), mace (*javetri*), saffron (*kesar*), black cardamoms (*moti elaichi*), green cardamoms (*chhoti elaichi*), fennel seeds (*saunf*), cinnamon (*dalchini*), royal cumin (*shah jeera*) etc. The curries are grouped on the basis of their colour – Red, Yellow, Green, White and Brown. Although a green curry will not always be a perfect green, but it will certainly have a hint of green in it. Similarly, a white curry will not be pure white as it will take some colour from the spices added to it. This division is done to make your table spread look attractive when you serve a meal. Enjoy a variety of flavours with your friends and family!

Nita Mehta

CONTENTS

Introduction   3

YELLOW CURRIES   5

Achaari Paneer 6
Rajasthani Gatta Curry............................. 7
Delicious Vegetable Korma..................... 8
Capsicums in Sesame Curry 10
Kandhari Khumb 11
Mughlai Dum Aloo 12

RED CURRIES   13

Mirchon Ki Sabzi................................... 14
 Soya Gravy.. 15
Makhmali Paneer 16
Angeethi Tamaatar................................ 17
Water Melon Curry 18
Laal Makai 19
Kofta Rangeen 20
 Shahi Paneer 22
Akbari Mushrooms................................ 24
Methi Malai Paneer.............................. 25

GREEN CURRIES   26

Saunf waale Parwal............................... 27
Dhania Matar 28
Healthy Broccoli Curry........................... 29
Besani Pakodi in Spinach Gravy............. 30
Pista Paneer 31

WHITE CURRIES   32

Broccoli & Corn Kofta 33
Paneer Laung Latika.............................. 35
Kashmiri Nadru Yakhni 36
Avadhi Kebabs in Shahi Gravy............... 38
Lajawab Baingan.................................. 39

BROWN CURRIES   40

Kashmiri Dum Aloo............................... 41
Soya Chunks with Capsicum.................. 42
Chettinad Curry 43
Goan Mushroom Xacutti 44
Tiranga Paneer ka Salan 46
Vegetable Sticks in Curry 47

INTERNATIONAL CONVERSION GUIDE   48

SIMPLY DELICIOUS

YELLOW
CURRIES

Achaari Paneer

Serves 6-8

INGREDIENTS

300 gms paneer - cut into 1½" cubes
2 capsicums - cut into ½" pieces
½" piece ginger & 5-6 flakes garlic - crushed
to a paste (2 tsp paste)
1 cup curd - beat well till smooth
4 tbsp oil
3 onions - chopped finely
4 green chillies - chopped
½ tsp turmeric (*haldi*) powder
¾ tsp garam masala
1 tsp amchoor (dried mango powder) or
lemon juice to taste
2-3 green chillies - cut lengthwise into 4 pieces
1 tsp salt or to taste
½ cup milk mixed with ½ cup water
½ cup cream

ACHAARI MASALA (KEEP TOGETHER)
2 tsp aniseeds (*saunf*)
¾ tsp mustard seeds (*rai*)
a pinch of fenugreek seeds (*methi daana*)
½ tsp onion seeds (*kalonji*)
1 tsp cumin seeds (*jeera*)

1. Cut paneer into 1½" cubes. Rub ½ tsp turmeric, a pinch of salt and ½ tsp red chilli powder on the paneer and capsicum. Keep aside for 10 minutes.

2. Heat oil. Add the achaari masala together to the hot oil. Let them crackle for 1 minute or till cumin turns golden.

3. Add onions and chopped green chillies. Cook till onions turn golden. Add turmeric and garlic-ginger paste. Stir.

4. Beat curd with ¼ cup water and a pinch of turmeric till smooth. Add gradually & keep stirring. Add dry mango powder, garam masala and ¾ tsp salt. Cook for 2-3 minutes on low heat till the curd dries up a little. (Do not make it very dry). Remove from fire and let it cool down.

5. At the time of serving, add milk mixed with water and slit green chillies to the cold masala and mix well. Boil on low heat for a minute, stirring continuously. Add capsicum. Simmer for 2-3 minutes. Add cream and paneer cubes, cook for a minute on low flame. Serve hot.

Rajasthani Gatta Curry

Serves 4-5

INGREDIENTS

GATTE
1 cup gramflour (*besan*)
a pinch of baking soda (*mitha soda*)
½ tsp carom seeds (*ajwain*)
½ tsp turmeric (*haldi*), ½ tsp red chilli powder
1 tsp salt, ½ tsp cumin (*jeera*) powder
½ tsp fennel (*saunf*) - coarsely powdered
½ tsp coriander (*dhania*) powder
½ tsp garam masala powder
½ tsp ginger paste, ½ tsp green chilli paste
3 tsp malai or cream, 2 tbsp curd

CURRY (MIX TOGETHER)
1 cup curd (preferably 1-2 days old)
2 tsp gram flour (*besan*)
½ tsp turmeric (*haldi*) powder, 1½ tsp salt
½ tsp red chilli powder
½ tsp ginger paste
½ tsp cumin (*jeera*), 3-4 cloves (*laung*)
2 black cardamoms (*moti elaichi*)
2 medium tomatoes - pureed and strained
3 tbsp oil
some fresh coriander - for garnishing

1. For making gatte, mix together all ingredients to get a soft dough like a chappati dough. Add more curd if required to get a soft dough. Do not add any water. With the help of oil smeared on your hands, roll out thin fingers 3"- 4" long, like cylinders.

2. Boil 5 cups of water. Keep the gatte in a stainless steel round strainer and keep the strainer on a pan of boiling water and cover with a lid. Steam gatte for 5-7 minutes. Remove from fire. Let them cool. Later cut them into rounds of ¾" thickness. Keep aside.

3. For curry, mix together curd, gramflour, turmeric, salt & ginger paste. Add 1 cup water. Beat well and strain.

4. Heat oil. Add cumin, cloves & cardamoms. Fry for 1 minute.

5. Add red chilli powder and the curd mixture. Go on stirring till it boils.

6. Add pureed tomatoes (should be very smooth, so strain to make it smooth). Give 2-3 boils. Add gatte (can add more water if more gravy is needed). Cover, lower heat. Simmer for 4-5 minutes. Serve hot garnished with fresh coriander.

Delicious Vegetable Korma

Serves 4

INGREDIENTS

1 potato, 1 carrot, 1 gaanth gobi or knol-khol
10-12 french beans, ½ cup peas
½ small cauliflower, 2 tbsp oil, 2 tsp ghee
3-4 green chillies - slit, 2 sprigs curry leaves
2 onions - chopped
2 tomatoes - chopped
½ tsp turmeric powder (*haldi*)
½-1 tsp chilli powder, or to taste
2 tsp coriander powder, 1 tsp salt to taste

SEASONINGS

2 bay leaves (*tej patta*), 6 cloves (*laung*)
3-4 big cardamoms (*elaichi*)
2 tsp aniseeds (*saunf*)

GRIND TO PASTE

2 tsp chopped ginger, 6-8 flakes garlic
2-3 green chillies

COCONUT PASTE

6-8 tbsp grated fresh coconut
6-8 cashew nuts
3 tsp poppy seeds (*khus-khus*)
1 tbsp chopped coriander

5. Now add chopped tomato and continue to saute till they turn soft. Add turmeric powder, red chilli powder, coriander powder and salt. Stir all the while, till oil surfaces.

6. Now add the vegetables, saute for 5 minutes.

7. Add coconut paste and saute for a minute. Add 1½-2 cups water, mix, cover and cook on low heat till the gravy is well blended and the vegtables are cooked. Remove from heat, pour into a bowl.

8. Garnish with chopped coriander leaves and fried cashew nuts. Serve hot with puris, plain rice or aapam.

1. Wash, peel and cut potato, carrot and knol-khol into small pieces of desired size. String and cut beans, break cauliflower into small florets.

2. For coconut paste, grind fresh coconut with cashews, poppy seeds & coriander with some water to a smooth paste.

3. Heat oil-ghee together, add add bay leaf, cloves, cardamoms and aniseeds. Wait for 30 seconds to get fragrant. Add slit chillies, curry leaves & chopped onions. Fry till onions are brown.

4. Add ginger-garlic-green chilli paste and sauté on low heat for sometime.

Capsicums in Sesame Curry

Serves 4

3 tbsp sesame seeds (*til*) - roasted on a tawa
till it starts to change colour
2 tbsp desiccated coconut (*nariyal ka bura*)
4 tbsp curd
2 green capsicums - sliced into thin fingers
2 potatoes - cut into small cubes and boiled in
salted water (1 cup), 1 tsp cumin seeds (*jeera*)
2 onions - finely chopped
1 tbsp tomato ketchup
4- 5 fresh green chillies - chopped finely
1¼ tsp salt, ½ tsp turmeric (*haldi*)
¼-½ tsp red chilli powder
½ tsp sugar, 5 tbsp oil

1. Grind coconut and sesame seeds in a grinder with 4 tbsp curd to a fine paste.

2. Heat 3 tbsp oil in a kadhai, add cumin seeds. Wait till golden.

3. Add onions and fry till golden brown in colour.

4. Add turmeric, salt & chilli powder. Stir.

5. Add the potatoes and coconut-sesame paste. Bhuno and cook till oil separates. Sprinkle some water in between if the paste sticks to the sides of the kadhai.

6. Add tomato ketchup and green chillies. Stir.

7. Add 2½ cups of water and sugar. Give 2-3 boils. Simmer for 3-4 minutes. Remove from fire.

8. Heat 2 tbsp oil in a pan or kadhai, add sliced capsicum and stir fry them for a few minutes or till they get brown patches & get slightly wilted or soft. Sprinkle ¼ tsp salt and mix. Keep aside till serving time.

9. At serving time, heat gravy and add fried capsicums. Mix well, cook for a minute. Serve hot.

Kandhari Khumb

Serves 6

200 gm mushrooms (12-15 big size pieces)
juice of ½ lemon, 2 tsp salt
1 tbsp butter - melted

FILLING
50 gms khoya or cheese - grated
1 small onion - chopped
½" piece ginger - grated
3-4 cashews - very finely chopped
3 tbsp anaar ke dane
3 tbsp chopped coriander
½ tsp garam masala, ½ tsp black pepper
½ tsp roasted cumin (*bhuna jeera*) powder
2-3 big pinches of salt

GRAVY
1 cup fresh pomegranate (*anaar ke dane*)
3 onions, 1 tbsp chopped ginger
4 dry red chillies
4 tbsp oil
4-5 green cardamoms (*elaichi*) - pounded to
open slightly
½ tsp garam masala, ½ tsp red chilli powder
½ tsp turmeric (*haldi*)
1 tsp coriander (*dhania*) powder
1½ tsp salt or to taste
1 cup milk

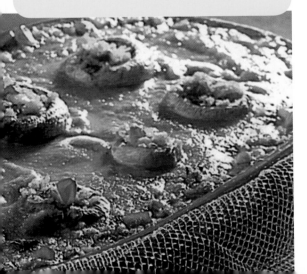

1. Wash mushrooms and pull out the stalks. Hollow the mushrooms a little more with the help of a small scooper. Keep stalks aside to use for pullao or soup!

2. Boil 4-5 cups water with 2 tsp salt and juice of ½ lemon. Add the mushrooms. Boil for 2 minutes. Drain and refresh with cold water. Strain. Wipe to dry well. Brush mushrooms with melted butter.

3. For filling - heat oil in a kadhai, add onion, cook till soft. Remove from fire. Mix all the other ingredients given under filling.

4. Stuff each mushroom with it. Place the mushrooms in a hot oven at 220°C for 5 minutes. Remove from oven.

5. To prepare the gravy, blend the anaar ke daane with 1½ cups water in a mixer blender. Strain to get juice.

6. Grind onions, ginger and dry red chillies to a fine paste.

7. Heat 4 tbsp oil in a heavy kadhai. Add green cardamoms. Wait for a minute. Add the onion paste. Cook on low flame for about 4-5 minutes till onions turn golden. Add masalas - garam masala, red chilli powder, turmeric, coriander & salt. Stir. Add anaar juice. Boil, simmer for 3-4 minutes. Remove from fire. Cool.

8. To serve, add milk to the cold gravy. Simmer on low flame for 5 minutes. Pour in a serving dish. Arrange mushrooms on it. Heat in a microwave or oven. Serve.

KANDHARI PANEER

You can put paneer pieces in the same gravy

Mughlai Dum Aloo

Serves 4-5

INGREDIENTS

2 cups (250 gms) baby potatoes – boiled & peeled
2 big tomatoes - pureed
2 tbsp tomato puree (ready-made)
50 gms khoya – grated (1/3 cup)
½ tsp turmeric (*haldi*) powder
1½ tsp salt
2 tbsp cream, 2 tbsp curd
1 tsp lemon juice, or to taste
½ tsp chaat masala

PASTE (GRIND TOGETHER)

2 tbsp coriander seeds (*sabut dhania*)
½" piece of ginger, 1 green chilli
½ tsp cumin seeds (*jeera*)
7-8 cashewnuts
2-3 black pepper corns (*saboot kali mirch*)
2 green cardamom (*chhoti elaichi*)
1 black cardamom (*moti elaichi*)
2 cloves (*laung*), 1-2 cinnamon (*dalchini*)
1-2 mace blades (*javitri*), 2 dry red chillies

TEMPERING

4 tbsp ghee
1 tsp royal cumin seeds (*shah jeera*)

1. Mix all the ingredients of the paste in a bowl, soak in ¼ cup water for ½ an hour. Grind to a smooth paste. Add ¾ cup water to make it thin.

2. Heat ghee in a pan. Add royal cumin seeds, when it splutters add the masala paste. Sauté for 3-4 minutes.

3. Add grated khoya, saute for 1-2 minutes. Add pureed tomatoes and tomato puree, turmeric, salt and chaat masala and mix well. Saute for 5-7 minutes. Keep stirring continuously till oil separates. Now remove from fire. Let it cool completely.

4. Add curd and cream and mix well. Again keep on low flame and cook for 1-2 minutes.

5. Add potatoes in the masala and cook for 1-2 minutes. Put 2 cups of water to get a thick gravy. Give a boil and cook on low heat for 2-3 minutes. Add lemon juice if needed. Garnish with coriander leaves.

SIMPLY DELICIOUS

RED
CURRIES

Mirchon Ki Sabzi

Serves 4-5

INGREDIENTS

9-10 thick green chilies (*achaari mirch*)
6 potatoes – boiled and mashed
1 tsp salt or to taste, 1½ tsp chaat masala
½ tsp dry mango powder (*amchoor*)
½ red chilli powder, ¼ tsp garam masala
2 tbsp curd, 1 tsp lemon juice
a pinch of black salt (*kala namak*)
½ tsp butter

GRAVY

4 tomatoes – boil in water for 3-4 minutes,
peel and grind to a fine paste
½ tsp salt or to taste
a pinch of dry mango powder (*amchoor*)
1 tbsp curd, 2 tbsp cream
¼ tsp red chilli powder
¼ tsp turmeric (*haldi*) powder
¼ tsp garam masala, ½ tsp chaat masala
2 tbsp ghee, 1 tsp cumin seeds (*jeera*)
1½ cups water

1. Slit and deseed green chillies. Boil water in a pan. Put green chillies in the boiling water and remove from fire. Take out green chillies from water after a minute.

2. In a pan heat butter. Add potatoes, salt, chaat masala, dry mango powder, red chili powder, garam masala, curd, lemon juice and kala namak. Sauté on low heat for 5 minutes to prepare a nice masala. Remove from fire and cool.

3. Fill each green chilli with this masala nicely.

4. For gravy, heat ghee in a pan, add cumin seeds. When it splutters add pureed tomatoes, salt, dry mango powder, garam masala, chaat masala, turmeric powder and red chili powder. Saute for 7-8 minutes.

5. Add curd & cream. Saute for 2-3 minutes. If there is any filling remaining, add filling in the gravy masala and mix well.

6. Sauté masala till it leaves oil. Add the stuffed green chillies and put 1 cup water to get a thick gravy. Cover and Cook on low heat.

7. When the green chilies are cooked remove from fire and serve.

Soya Gravy

Serves 4

INGREDIENTS

1 cup soya nutri granules
2 potatoes - cut into ½" cubes
1 cup peas - boiled
1-2 tsp lemon juice
4 tbsp ghee/oil
2 cloves (*laung*)
2 onions - chopped roughly
4 tomatoes - each cut into half
1 whole dry red chilli - broken into pieces
½ tsp cumin seeds (*jeera*)
2-3 green cardamoms - slighlty hit to open
½ tsp garm masala
¼ tsp turmeric (*haldi*)
1 tbsp coriander (*dhania*) powder
1 tsp salt
½ tsp degi mirch powder
1 tsp tandoori masala
½ tsp dry mango powder (*amchoor*)
2 tsp ginger-garlic paste

4. Add the nutri granules and bhuno for 1-2 minutes. Add all the dry masala powders. Bhuno for 2 minutes. Add 2 cups water. Give one boil. Simmer for 5 minutes till a thick masala gravy is ready. Add tandoori masala & dry mango powder. Mix well. Remove from fire.

5. Peel and slice the potato into ½" thick round slices. Cut slices into small cubes. Deep fry potato cubes till golden and cooked on low medium flame

6. Add fried potatoes and boiled peas to the masala gravy and bring to a boil. Simmer for 2-3 minutes. Serve hot.

1. Boil 3-4 cups water with 1 tsp salt, juice of ½ lemon. Add nutri granules and boil for 2-3 minutes. Strain.

2. Heat 2 tbsp ghee/oil in a pressure cooker, add cloves, dry red chilli, onions. Stir till soft. Add tomatoes. Cook for 4-5 minutes. Add 1 cup water and pressure cook to give 2 whistles. Remove from fire and let it cool completely. Puree in a grinder to a smooth paste.

3. Heat 2 tbsp oil in a kadhai. Add cumin seeds and green cardamoms. Wait till cumin turns golden. Add fresh tomato puree and cook till dry. Add ginger-garlic paste and cook till oil separates.

Makhmali Paneer

Serves 4-5

INGREDIENTS

200 gm paneer - cut into pieces
½ cup coconut milk, fresh/ready made, see
note, ½ tsp sugar - optional
4 large tomatoes - chopped roughly
2 green chillies - chopped roughly
1 tbsp chopped ginger
8-10 flakes garlic - chopped
1 tsp salt, or to taste

BAGHAR/TEMPERING
2 tbsp ghee or oil
1 tsp black mustard seeds (*sarson*)
2 whole, dry red chillies
10-15 curry leaves/coriander leaves

1. Roughly chop the tomatoes and green chillies. In a pressure cooker, cook together tomatoes, green chillies, ginger, garlic and salt with 1 cup water on high flame to give 2 whistles.

2. After the pressure drops, cool and make a very smooth puree in a mixer-grinder. Put the tomato puree back in the pressure cooker.

3. Add the coconut milk to it. Boil on low heat. Simmer for a minute.

4. Add the paneer pieces to it. Simmer for 4-5 minutes till gravy turns a little thick. Add sugar if the gravy tastes too sour.

5. Transfer the paneer to a serving dish.

6. Heat 2 tbsp ghee or oil for tempering. Reduce heat. Add mustard seeds and let them crackle. Add whole red chillies and curry leaves. Remove from fire when chilles darken.

7. Pour the ghee over the paneer in the serving dish.

Note: You may use desiccated coconut powder instead of coconut milk. Simply fill ½ cup with desiccated coconut and fill the cup with warm water. Mix well and use instead of coconut milk. To take out fresh coconut milk, put 1 cup hot water on ½ cup freshly grated coconut. Keep aside for 15 minutes. Blend it in a blender and strain through a muslin cloth to get fresh coconut milk.

Angeethi Tamaatar

Serves 6

INGREDIENTS

6 small firm tomatoes, 2-3 tbsp oil

FILLING

150 gms paneer - grated (1½ cups)
1 tbsp roasted peanuts - roughly crushed
2-3 tbsp corn - boiled
1-2 tbsp chopped coriander
1 green chilli - deseeded and chopped
½ tsp chaat masala
½ tsp salt or to taste, ½ tsp garam masala
a pinch of black salt

GRAVY

2 big onions, 1 tbsp chopped ginger
½ cup curd, ½ tsp turmeric (*haldi*)
1 tsp coriander (*dhania*) powder
½ tsp chilli powder, ¾ tsp salt
½ tsp garam masala, 1 tbsp tomato ketchup
1 tbsp chopped fresh coriander

1. Rub a little oil over the tomatoes and roast on a naked flame. Roast on low flame for 2-3 minutes, changing sides till tomatoes become a little soft. Let them get charred (blackened) at some places. Keep aside. Let them cool.

2. Slice a small piece from the top of each tomato. Scoop out carefully, (to make place for filling). Keep the scooped tomato pulp aside for the gravy.

3. Rub some salt on the inside of tomatoes & keep them upside down for 10 minutes.

4. Grate paneer. Add all other ingredients of the filling & mix gently. Do not mash.

5. Fill the scooped & roasted tomatoes with the filling. Press well. Keep the left over filling (2 tbsp) aside for the gravy.

6. To prepare the gravy, grind onions, ginger and the scooped out portion of the tomatoes together.

7. Heat 3- 4 tbsp oil. Add the onion-tomato paste and cook till oil separates.

8. Beat curd lightly with a fork and add gradually to the above masala. Cook on low flame till the masala turns dry.

9. Add turmeric, coriander powder, chilli powder, salt & garam masala. Cook for 1 minute.

10. Add 1½ cups hot water and tomato ketchup to get a thick gravy. Boil. Simmer on low flame for 7- 8 minutes, till oil separates.

11. Add left over paneer of the filling (2 tbsp) & coriander. Mix well. Keep aside.

12. To serve, put some hot gravy in a serving dish. Heat stuffed tomatoes in an oven and arrange on the hot gravy. Sprinkle some hot gravy on the top also. If you have a microwave, then arrange tomatoes on gravy in a serving dish and heat together.

Water Melon Curry

Serves 4

INGREDIENTS

4 cups of tarbooz (water melon) - cut into
1" pieces along with a little white portion
also, and deseeded
4-5 flakes garlic - crushed
2 tbsp oil
½ tsp cumin seeds (*jeera*)
a pinch of asafoetida (*hing*)
1 tsp gram flour (*besan*)
1 tbsp ginger - cut into thin match sticks
(jullienes)
½ tsp coriander (*dhania*) powder
½ - ¾ tsp chilli powder
a pinch of turmeric (*haldi*) powder
½ tsp salt, or to taste
2 tsp lemon juice

GARNISH
sliced green chillies
chopped green coriander

1. Puree 1½ cups of water melon cubes (the upper soft red pieces) with 4-5 flakes of garlic to get 1 cup of water melon puree. Leave the remaining firm, lower pieces with the white portion as it is. Keep aside.

2. Heat oil in a kadhai or a pan. Add asafoetida and cumin Let cumin turn golden. Add 1 tsp gramflour. Stir for 1-2 minutes on low heat till golden and fragrant.

3. Add garlic and shredded ginger and stir for ½ minute.

4. Add the remaining firm, water melon pieces and stir to mix.

5. Sprinkle coriander powder, red chilli powder and turmeric. Stir for ½ minute.

6. Add the water melon puree, salt and lemon juice. Simmer for 2-3 minutes till you get a thin curry. Remove from fire.

7. Garnish with green chillies and green coriander. Serve hot with boiled rice.

Laal Makai

Serves 5-6

INGREDIENTS

200 gm baby corns - keep whole or cut lengthwise into half if thick
4 -5 kashmiri dry red chillies - soak in ¼ cup water and grind to a paste
2 tsp ginger-garlic paste
2 black cardamoms (*moti elaichi*)
2 laung (*cloves*), 1" cinnamon (*dalchini*)
3 onions - chopped finely
1 tsp degi mirch powder
1 cup yogurt, 1 tsp cumin powder
¼ tsp of turmeric (*haldi*)
1 tsp coriander (*dhania*) powder
½ tsp garam masala
½ tsp sugar, salt to taste

1. Boil 4 cups water with 1 tbsp lemon juice, 1 tsp salt and 1 tsp sugar. Add baby corns and boil for 3-4 minutes till soft. Remove fromwater and keep aside.

2. Heat 4 tbsp oil. Add cardamoms, cloves and cinnamon. Wait for a minute till fragrant. Add onions & saute till golden

3. Add baby corns & saute for 2-3 minutes. Add degi mirch powder and stir to mix well.

4. Add dry red chilli paste and garlic-ginger paste and mix well.

5. Beat yogurt and mix cumin powder, turmeric, coriander powder and garam masala. Add yogurt to baby corns. Stir nicely for 4-5 minutes till dry and oil separates. Add salt to taste.

6. Add 1½ cups water. Bring to a boil and simmer covered for 3-4 minutes. Add ½ tsp sugar, if needed. Serve with rice or roti.

Kofta Rangeen

Makes 6

KOFTA COVERING

4 slices bread - dipped in water & squeezed
4 potatoes - boiled & grated (2 cups)
¾ tsp salt, or to taste
½ tsp black pepper
pinch of baking powder
2 tsp tomato ketchup

KOFTA FILLING

1 carrot - grated finely (½ cup)
1 capsicum - thin, 1" long pieces (½ cup)
3-4 tbsp grated green cabbage
¼ cup grated cheese
salt, pepper to taste

GRAVY

4 tbsp oil, 2 black cardamoms (*elaichi*)
2 onions - chopped (1 cup)
3 tomatoes - chopped (1½ cups)
2 tsp chopped ginger
1½ tsp coriander (*dhania*) powder
½ tsp each red chilli powder & garam masala
¾ cup milk
1 tbsp tomato ketchup
salt to taste

1. For the kofta covering, in a bowl mix potatoes with all the ingredients till well blended. Divide into 6 balls. Keep aside

2. For the filling, mix all the vegetables with cheese together. Sprinkle some salt and pepper to taste.

3. Flatten each potato ball. Place 1 tbsp of filling in the centre. Lift the sides to cover the filling. Roll between the palms to make it smooth. Deep fry koftas, one at a time, carefully till golden brown.

4. To prepare the gravy, grind onions, tomatoes and ginger together.

5. Heat oil. Add cardamoms and wait for 30-40 seconds. Add onion-tomato paste and cook on medium heat till well dried. Add ground coriander and red chilli powder. Stir fry till oil comes to the surface.

6. Reduce heat. Add milk gradually, 2-3 tbsp at a time, stirring continuously till all the milk is used. Cook on low heat till the mixture turns red again and the oil separates. Add enough water to get a thin curry. Boil. Add salt, garam masala, tomato ketchup and cook on low heat for 8-10 minutes till it thickens slightly. Keep aside.

7. To serve, cut koftas into two. Boil the gravy separately, and pour in a serving dish. Arrange the koftas on the gravy and microwave for 1-2 minutes to heat the koftas. Serve immediately.

Shahi Paneer

Serves 4

INGREDIENTS

200 gms paneer - cut into 1" cubes
4 tomatoes - chopped roughly
2 tbsp oil
1 tbsp ghee
4 onions - chopped roughly
1 tsp chopped ginger
1 tsp chopped garlic
¾ tsp paneer masala or garam masala
1 tsp salt or to taste
2 tbsp cashews (*kaju*)
1-2 dry red chillies - deseeded
1 tbsp dry fenugreek leaves (*kasoori methi*)
½ cup milk
1 cup water
3-4 tbsp cream

1. Boil cashews and dry red chillies in ½ cup water for 2 minutes. Drain & grind to a very smooth paste. Keep aside.

2. Heat oil in a kadhai. Add onions, chopped ginger and garlic. Cook till onions turn golden brown. Remove from fire. Let it cool.

3. Grind tomatoes to a puree in a mixer grinder. Add the cooled onions to the tomatoes in the mixer grinder and grind all together to a paste.

4. Heat 1 tbsp ghee. Add the paste and cook till dry. Add dry fenugreek leaves, paneer masala or garam masala and salt. Cook till oil separates.

5. Add cashew-red chilli paste and stir for a minute. Add 1 cup water. Bring to a boil and simmer for 2-3 minutes. Remove from fire and let it cool down.

6. At the time of serving, add milk to the cold masala and mix well. Boil on low heat, stirring continuously. Add paneer. Simmer for 2-3 minutes.

7. Add cream and mix. Serve.

Akbari Mushrooms

Serves 8

INGREDIENTS

200 gm mushrooms
juice of ½ lemon, 1 tsp salt
1 tbsp butter, ¼ tsp pepper
1 tbsp oil, 10-12 cashews - split

GRIND TOGETHER

2 small onions, 4 tomatoes
1 tbsp chopped ginger, 1 green chilli

ALMOND PASTE

2 tbsp almonds - boiled for 2-3 minutes in
water, peeled and ground with ¼ cup water

OTHER INGREDIENTS

4 tbsp oil
½ tsp royal cumin (*shah jeera*)
½ tsp red chilli powder
1 tsp coriander (*dhania*) powder
½ tsp dry mango powder (*amchoor*)
1½ tsp salt, 1 tsp garam masala
1 cup milk, 1 tsp tandoori masala
seeds of 3 green cardamoms (*elaichi*), crushed
50-100 gms paneer - grated (½-1 cup)
3 tbsp chopped coriander

BAGHAR OR TEMPERING

1 tbsp oil, ½ tsp black cumin (*shah jeera*)
1 tsp finely chopped ginger
5-6 almonds - cut into thin long pieces
¼ tsp red chilli powder

1. Wash mushrooms. Keep mushrooms whole, cutting away the stalk. (use the stalks to make mushroom and peas pullao!)

2. Boil 4 cups water with 1 tsp salt and juice of ½ lemon. Add the whole mushrooms. Boil for 2 minutes. Drain and refresh with cold water. Wipe on a kitchen towel.

3. Heat 1 tbsp oil in a pan. Add cashews and stir till golden. Remove from pan.

4. Heat 1 tbsp butter and saute mushrooms on high heat till dry. Sprinkle pepper and mix. Remove from fire.

5. For the curry, heat oil. Add royal cumin. After a minute, add onion-tomato paste and cook till dry and oil separates. Reduce flame. Add red chilli powder, coriander, dry mango powder, salt and garam masala. Cook for 1 minute.

6. Add almond paste. Stir to mix well.

7. Keeping the flame low, add milk, stirring continuously. Stir for 2-3 minutes.

8. Add enough (2-3 cups approx.) water to get a thin gravy. Boil.

9. Add mushrooms and simmer for 2-3 minutes till slightly thick. Add tandoori masala, cardamom powder, grated paneer and fresh coriander.

10. Transfer to a serving dish. Heat oil. Add black cumin and ginger. After a few seconds, add almonds and stir. Add red chilli powder, remove from fire and pour tempering on the gravy. Serve.

Akbari Mushrooms with corn and peas
Add some boiled peas and corn to the gravy

Methi Malai Paneer

Serves 4

INGREDIENTS

200 gms paneer - cut into 1½" fingers
¾ cup frozen or boiled peas
3 tbsp oil
¼ tsp pepper powder
2 tbsp malai or cream - whisk with
¼ cup milk till smooth
3 tbsp dry fenugreek leaves (*kasoori methi*)
1 tsp salt, or to taste
a pinch of dry mango powder (*amchoor*)
¼ tsp red chilli powder
1 cup water

ONION PASTE
½" stick cinnamon (*dalchini*)
seeds of 2 cardamoms (*moti elaichi*)
3 cloves (*laung*), 1 large onion
½" piece ginger - chopped

TOMATO-KAJU PASTE
1 large tomato - chopped
2 tbsp (8-10) cashewnuts (*kaju*)
1 green chilli - chopped

1. For the onion paste, grind together onion, cinnamon, cloves, seeds of cardamoms and ginger in a mixer grinder with a little water. Keep aside.

2. For the tomato-kaju paste, grind together tomato, cashews and 1 green chilli. Keep aside.

3. Heat oil. Add onion paste and cook on low heat till oil separates. Do not let the onion turn brown.

4. Add tomato paste. Cook till dry and oil separates

5. Add dry fenugreek leaves, salt, dry mango powder and chilli powder. Add peas and stir for 2 minutes.

6. Add malai whisked with milk, cook on low heat for 2-3 minutes till malai dries up slightly.

7. Add enough water, about one cup, to get a thick gravy. Boil for 2-3 minutes.

8. Add paneer. Bring to a boil. Add pepper powder. Remove from fire.

9. Serve garnished with some cashewnut bits, roasted on a tawa till golden.

SIMPLY DELICIOUS

GREEN
CURRIES

Saunf waale Parwal

Serves 4

INGREDIENTS

250 gm tender parwals - scraped lightly & slit

FILLING - ONION PASTE
3 tsp fennel (*saunf*)
2 onions - chopped
2 tsp coriander (*dhania*) powder
½ tsp red chilli powder
½ tsp garam masala
½ tsp dry mango powder (*amchoor*)

GREEN CURD PASTE
2 cups curd
1 tbsp chopped ginger
2 green chillies
1 cup fresh coriander
½ tsp salt

OTHER INGREDIENTS
1 tsp cumin (*jeera*)
3 whole, dry red chillies
2 tsp gram flour (*besan*)

1. Grind chopped onions and fennel to a paste.

2. Grind coriander, ginger, green chilli, curd & salt to a green paste. Keep aside.

3. For the filling, heat 1 tbsp oil. Add fennel and onion paste. Cook till onions turn light brown. Add coriander powder, red chilli powder, garam masala, dry mango powder and ¼ tsp salt. Mix well and remove from fire.

4. Peel parwals lightly to keep them crunchy. Make a lengthwise cut and remove hard seeds if any. Fill the onion mixture into the slit parwals.

5. Heat 2 tbsp oil in flat pan and stir fry stuffed parwals for 3-4 minutes. Sprinkle ½ tsp salt. Cover and cook on low flame till tender. Keep aside.

6. Heat 1 tbsp oil. Add cumin and dry red chillies. Let cumin turn golden.

7. Remove from fire. Add gramflour and stir for a minute. Add green curd paste, stirring continuously. Return to low heat and bring to a boil, stirring constantly. Simmer for 2 minutes on low flame.

8. To serve, boil curry in a flat pan and add parwals. Simmer for 2 minutes. Serve.

Dhania Matar

Serves 4-5

INGREDIENTS

2 cups peas - boil in salted water till soft
2-3 tbsp oil
a pinch of asafoetida (*hing*)
1 tsp cumin seeds (*jeera*)
½ tsp onion seeds (*kalonji*)
2 tbsp cashewnuts - boiled in ¼ cup water,
cooled and ground to a paste
1 firm tomato - cut into 8 pieces, deseeded
½ tsp garam masala

DHANIA CHUTNEY
2 cups chopped coriander leaves
4 flakes garlic - chopped
1 tbsp chopped ginger, 2 green chillies
1 tomato - chopped
¾ tsp salt, or to taste
¼ tsp lemon juice

1. Grind together all the ingredients of the dhania chutney.

2. Heat 3 tbsp oil in a pan. Add asafoetida, cumin & onion seeds.

3. When cumin turns golden, add peas. Saute for 2 minutes.

4. Add dhania chutney to the peas and cook till dry.

5. Add cashew paste. Stir to mix well. Add enough water, about 1 cup, to get a gravy. Boil. Simmer for 2-3 minutes. Check salt & add some more if needed.

6. Add tomato pieces and ½ tsp garam masala. Mix well. Serve hot.

Healthy Broccoli Curry

Serves 4-5

INGREDIENTS

1 medium flower of broccoli
1 carrot - cut into ¼" thick slices
juice of ½ lemon, 1 tbsp oil

CURRY

1 small flower (100 gm) of broccoli
2 green chillies, 2 cups milk
2 onions - ground to a paste
3 tbsp oil, 1 tsp cumin (*jeera*)
¼ tsp carom seeds (*ajwain*)
1 tsp ginger-garlic paste
1 tsp gramflour (*besan*)
1½ tsp coriander (*dhania*) powder
1 tsp garam masala, a pinch of turmeric (*haldi*)
1 tsp salt or to taste, ½ tsp pepper or to taste
2 tbsp grated cheese/paneer, optional

1. Cut both flowers of broccoli into medium florets with some stalk.

2. Boil 5-6 cups water with 2 tsp salt, 1 tsp sugar and juice of ½ lemon. Add broccoli florets and carrots to boiling water. When a proper boils comes, remove from fire. Drain. Refresh in cold water. Strain. Pat dry on a kitchen towel.

3. Heat 1 tbsp oil. Add all the broccoli florets and carrots and saute for 3-4 minutes. Sprinkle some salt and pepper.

4. Divide into two portions. Grind one portion of broccoli and green chillies with 1 cup milk to a smooth green puree in a grinder.

5. For curry, heat 3 tbsp oil, add cumin and carom seeds. Let cumin turn golden. Add onion paste. Cook on low heat till oil separates. Do not let it turn brownish. Add ginger-garlic paste. Stir for a minute. Add gramflour, coriander powder, garam masala, turmeric and salt to taste. Stir for 1 minute. Add pureed broccoli. Cook, stirring on low heat till oil separates.

6. Add 1 cup milk, stirring continuously. Stir till it boils. Cook for 2 minutes. Add ½ cup water to thin down the gravy. Do not make it too thin. Add pepper to taste. Boil. Simmer for a minute. Remove from fire. Add cheese if you like. Keep aside.

7. To serve, heat gravy and add sauted broccoli & carrots. Boil. Serve hot sprinkled with some cheese/paneer.

Besani Pakodi in Spinach Gravy

Serves 8-10

INGREDIENTS

1 bunch (600-700 gm) spinach - chopped
1 dry, red chilli
1 tbsp channa dal
½ tsp cumin (*jeera*)
¼ tsp mustard seeds (*rai*)
1 tbsp freshly grated coconut or
coconut powder
2 tbsp chopped fresh coriander
1-2 green chillies
3 tbsp oil
a pinch of asafoetida (*hing*)
¼ tsp fenugreek seeds (*methi dana*)
6-8 cashewnuts (*kaju*) - split
1 onion - chopped
1½ tsp salt, 1 tsp sugar
1 tsp full or ½ of a lemon size tamarind ball -
soak in ¼ cup warm water and squeeze
to get tamarind pulp

PAKORIS

4 tbsp gram flour (*besan*)
2 tsp semolina (*sooji*)
½ onion - chopped
½" piece ginger - chopped
2 tbsp green coriander - chopped
¼ tsp salt, ¼ tsp chilli powder
2 pinches baking powder

1. Clean, chop and wash spinach.

2. Roast red chilli, channa dal, cumin and mustard till cumin turns golden in a kadhai. Add coconut. Stir well and remove from fire. Grind all these ingredients with fresh coriander & green chillies to a fine paste. Keep masala paste aside.

3. Heat oil in a large kadhai. Add asafoetida and fenugreek seeds. Wait till fenugreek seeds turns brown. Add the cashewnuts and fry lightly till golden.

4. Add chopped onion and fry to a golden brown.

5. Add the masala paste. Mix well for a few seconds.

6. Add chopped spinach, salt and sugar. Cook for about 7-8 minutes till spinach turns soft. Remove from fire and cool.

7. Grind to a puree. Add tamarind pulp to the spinach. Boil. Add ½ cup water if too thick. Simmer for 3-4 minutes. Keep aside. Let it cool down.

8. For the pakoris, mix chopped onions, ginger, coriander, salt, chilli powder and baking powder with semolina and gramflour. Add a little water to make a thick batter. Beat well. Keep aside for 10 minutes. Deep fry small spoonfuls of the batter in medium hot oil.

9. Add pakoris to the cooled spinach. At serving time, give 2-3 boils.

Pista Paneer

Serves 6

INGREDIENTS

300 gm paneer - cut into 1" squares
2 large onions
2 tsp ginger-garlic paste or ½" ginger piece
and 6-8 flakes garlic - crushed to a paste
4 tbsp oil
2 tsp coriander (*dhania*) powder
½ tsp white pepper powder
1 tsp salt, or to taste
½ cup fresh cream
½ tsp garam masala powder

GRIND TOGETHER TO A PASTE
½ cup pistas alongwith the hard shell -
shelled, soaked and peeled
1 green chilli - finely chopped
½ cup chopped fresh coriander
½ cup yogurt

1. Peel and cut onions into 4 pieces. Boil in 1 cup water for 2-3 minutes. Drain, cool slightly and grind to a fine paste. Keep boiled onion paste aside.

2. Soak pistachio nuts in hot water for 10 minutes, drain and peel. Reserve a few peeled pistachio nuts for garnish.

3. Grind the remaining peeled pista with chopped green chillies and coriander to a fine green paste with yogurt.

4. Heat 4 tbsp oil in a kadhai, add boiled onion paste and saute for 7-8 minutes on low heat till dry and oil separates. See that the colour of the onions does not change to brown.

5. Add ginger-garlic paste and stir-fry for a minute. Add coriander powder, white pepper powder and salt and mix well.

6. Stir in the pista-green chilli paste and cook for 2-3 minutes on low heat till dry. Add 1½ cups water and bring to a boil. Simmer on low heat for 2-3 minutes.

7. Add paneer. Mix.

8. Stir in fresh cream, sprinkle garam masala powder and transfer to a serving dish. Sprinkle remaining pista nuts and some cream. Serve hot.

SIMPLY DELICIOUS

WHITE
C U R R I E S

Broccoli & Corn Kofta

Serves 4-6

INGREDIENTS

1 medium broccoli - grated finely along with tender stalks (2 cups grated)
1 potato - boiled and grated
4 tbsp frozen or boiled corn - chopped
1 tbsp roasted peanuts - crushed
¼ tsp coarsely crushed peppercorns (*saboot kali mirch*)
½ tsp salt, ¼ tsp garam masala
¼ tsp dry mango powder (*amchoor*)
1½ tbsp cornflour, a pinch of baking powder
½ tbsp butter

GRAVY

2 onions & 1 tbsp chopped ginger - ground to a paste together
2 tbsp cashew & 2 tbsp magaz (watermelon seeds) or 4 tbsp cashews - soaked in ½ cup hot water for 5 minutes
4 tbsp curd (yogurt)
3 tbsp oil
2 tsp dry fenugreek (*kasoori methi*)
1 tsp garam masala
½ tsp chilli powder
1¼ tsp salt, or to taste
½ cup milk
seeds of 3 green cardamoms (*elaichi*) - crushed
½ cup cream
2 tbsp corn - frozen or boiled

1. Grate the broccoli florets and the tender stems very finely.

2. Heat butter in a pan. Add grated broccoli. Add ¼ tsp salt. Stir on medium heat for 3-4 minutes on low heat. Remove from heat.

3. Grate the boiled potato. Add corn, peanuts, salt, crushed peppercorns, garam masala, mango powder, cornflour, baking powder and cooked broccoli to the potato. Mix well.

4. Make balls of the potato-broccoli mixture.

5. Deep fry 2-3 balls at a time till golden. Drain on absorbent paper.

6. For the gravy, drain cashewnuts and magaz, grind along with curd to a smooth paste.

7. Heat 3 tbsp oil. Add onion and ginger paste. Stir fry onion paste on low flame till oil separates and it turns transparent. Do not let it turn brown.

8. Gradually add curd-cashewnut mixture, stirring continuously. Stir for 4-5 minutes till masala turns thick and oil separates.

9. Add dry fenugreek, garam masala, red chilli powder & salt. Stir for 1-2 minutes.

10. Add 1½ cups water. Boil. Simmer for 2-3 minutes, on low flame, stirring constantly. Remove from fire and keep aside till serving time.

11. At serving time, add milk to get a thin gravy. Add crushed cardamoms. Keep on low heat & stir continuously till it boils.

12. Add cream and corn. Keep on low heat for 2-3 minutes. Add koftas. Simmer for a minute. Serve.

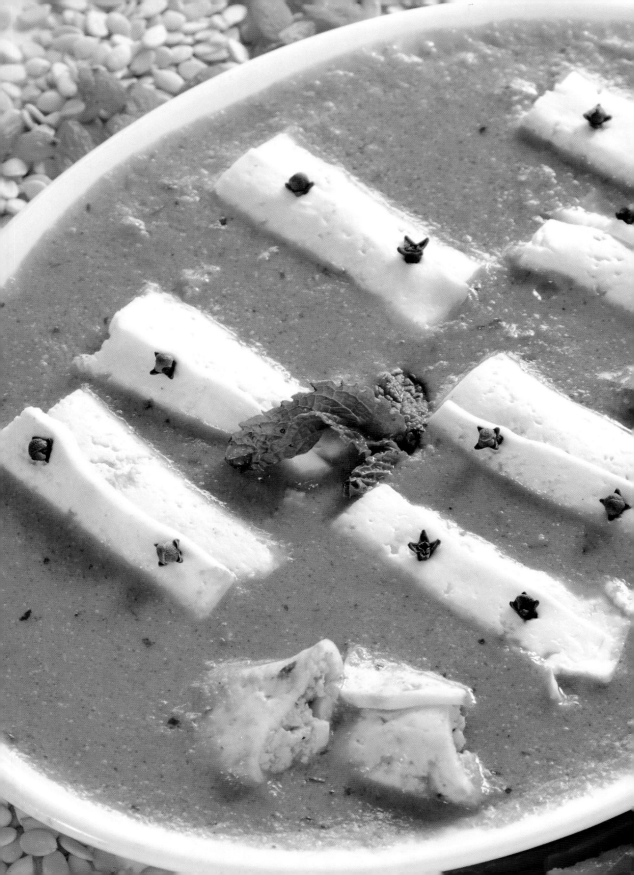

Paneer Laung Latika

Serves 8-10

INGREDIENTS

300 gm paneer - cut into very thin slices of 2"x1" rectangles
1 tbsp oil, ¼ tsp vinegar, ¼ tsp salt & pepper

FILLING
2 tbsp grated khoya/2tbsp cheese
1 tbsp each - chopped almonds & kishmish
½ green chilli -chopped
2-3 pinches each of - salt, garam masala, coriander powder, red chilli powder and pepper, all to taste

GRAVY
2 onions - deep fried till golden brown and ground to a paste
½ tsp red chilli powder, 1 tsp salt
1 tsp garam masala, a pinch of turmeric (*haldi*)
1 - 2 blades of star anise (*phool chakri*) - crushed to a powder
4 tbsp cream, 1 bay leaf (*tej patta*)
3 tbsp oil

GRIND TOGETHER
2 onions, 1 tsp chopped ginger
1 tsp chopped garlic, 1 green chilli

SOAK AND GRIND TOGETHER
8 almonds - soaked and peeled
3 tbsp melon seeds - soaked, ¼ cup curd

1. Cut paneer into very thin slices. Sprinkle oil, vinegar, pepper and salt on paneer and rub lightly to coat. Turn paneer and coat the other side. Keep aside to marinate for 5-10 minutes.

2. Pan fry paneer lightly on a greased pan till light golden on both sides. Take a slice and place it on a flat surface. Put a tbsp of filling at one end and roll up. Secure the joint with 2 cloves.

3. Heat oil in a kadhai. Add bay leaf. Wait for a minute. Add onion-ginger, garlic, chilli paste and stir till golden brown. Add red chilli powder, salt, garam masala and turmeric. Stir to mix. Add almond paste and stir for 2-3 minutes. Add 1½ cups water and bring to a boil. Simmer for 5-6 minutes on low heat.

4. Add fried onion paste and 2 pinches of star anise powder, or to taste. Simmer for 1-2 minutes. Add cream and bring to a slow boil. Remove from fire.

5. To serve, arrange paneer latika in hot gravy in a dish, microwave for 1 min.

Kashmiri Nadru Yakhni

Serves 4-5

INGREDIENTS

400 gms lotus stem (*nadru*)
4 tbsp oil
a pinch asafoetida (*hing*)
1-2 staranise (*phool chakri*), pic given below
4 cloves (*laung*)
6-7 peppercorns (*sabut kali mirch*)
1" cinnamon (*dalchini*)
1 black cardamom (*moti elaichi*)
3 cardamoms (*chhoti elaichi*) - pounded
1 bay leaf (*tej patta*)
½ tsp salt

MIX TOGETHER

1½ cups fresh yogurt - beaten well till smooth
1 tsp crushed fennel seeds (*saunf*)
crushed seeds of 1 black cardamom (*elaichi*)
1" cinnamon stick (*dalchini*) - crushed
½ tsp royal cumin (*shah jeera*) - crushed
½ tsp salt
1 tsp coriander powder (*dhania*)
1 tsp dry ginger powder (*sonth*)

TEMPERING

1-2 tbsp ghee
1 tsp royal cumin (*shah jeera*)
2 dry red chillies

1. Peel lotus stem. Cut diagonally into ¼" to ½" thick pieces. Clean the dirt if any with a tooth pick. Wash nicely.

2. Put in a pressure cook with ½ cup water. Add ½ tsp salt, asafoetida, star anise, cloves, peppercorns, cinnamon, bay leaf, cardamoms and black cardamom. Allow one whistle. Remove from heat and let it cool down.

3. In a kadhai heat 4 tbsp oil. Add cut lotus stems. Sauté for 4-5 minutes. Keep aside.

4. Whisk yogurt till smooth. Crush spices - fennel, seeds of black cardamom, cinnamon and royal cumin. Add these spices to the whisked yogurt. Also add salt, coriander powder and dry ginger powder to the yogurt.

5. Warm 2 tbsp oil in a pan on low heat. Add the yogurt mix and stir continuously on very low heat for 3-4 minutes till slightly thick.

6. Add the sautéd lotus stem slices. Stir for 3-4 minutes till done and some gravy remains. Remove from heat.

7. Heat 1 tbsp ghee. Reduce heat. Add royal cumin and dry red chillies. When the cumin turns golden, pour the ghee on top of the cooked lotus stem. Mix well and serve.

Avadhi Kebabs in Shahi Gravy

Serves 4-5

INGREDIENTS

KEBABS

250 gms potatoes - boiled and grated
¾ cup puffed lotus seeds (*makhane*)
8-10 almonds - finely chopped & roasted
¼ cup chopped coriander
½ cup chopped spinach
¼ cup cornflour, 1 tsp lemon juice
2 tbsp dry fenugreek leaves (*kasuri methi*)
½ tsp garam masala, ½ tsp red chilli powder
½ tsp salt, or to taste

MASALA PASTE (GRIND TOGETHER)

12 almonds, 4 tbsp melon seeds (*magaz*)
4 tbsp poppy seeds (*khus-khus*)
2-3 green chillies, 1 onion
½" piece of ginger, 3-4 flakes of garlic

OTHER INGREDIENTS

3 tbsp oil
2 onions - finely chopped
1 cup yogurt (*dahi*) - whisk till smooth
½ cup milk, ¼ cup cream
1 tsp sugar, 1 tsp salt

1. Heat 1 tbsp oil. Add makhanas and saute for 3-4 minutes. Remove from pan cool and crush with the hands roughly.

2. Dry roast the chopped almonds also till light golden. Remove from pan.

3. Mix all ingredients of the kebabs together. Form into 1½" long rolls and deep fry 1-2 at a time in hot oil. Keep aside.

4. For the gravy, heat 3 tbsp oil add chopped onions, stir till golden .Add the ground masala paste and fry for 2-3 minutes. Reduce heat, stirring continuously add yogurt, little at a time, stir till dry and oil separates. Add sugar and salt.

5. Add ½ cup water mixed with ½ cup milk, cook for another 3-4 minutes. Remove from heat & add cream.

6. At the time of serving heat up the gravy, add the kebabs and simmer for a minute for them to get hot. Serve hot.

Lajawab Baingan

Serves 4

INGREDIENTS

8 brinjals (small thin variety) - sliced to get
½" thick rounds and sprinkled with salt
3 onions - cut into 4 pieces
a lemon sized ball of tamarind (*imli*)
½ tsp mustard seeds (*sarson*)
½ tsp onion seeds (*kalonji*)
3 tbsp fresh cream

GRIND TOGETHER TO A SMOOTH PASTE

2 tbsp sesame seeds (*til*)
2 tbsp peanuts
6 flakes garlic, 1 tbsp chopped ginger
2 tsp coriander (*dhania*) powder
1 tsp cumin seeds (*jeera*)
½ tsp red chilli powder, 1 tsp salt

1. Cut onions roughly and boil in 3 cups water till soft. Drain and grind to a paste. Keep boiled onion paste aside.

2. Wash the tamarind and put in a bowl with 1½ cups hot water. Mash and leave it to soak for 10 minutes. Strain to extract juice.

3. Grind sesame seeds, peanuts, ginger, garlic, coriander, cumin seeds, red chilli powder and salt to a paste with a little water.

4. Pat dry the brinjals sprinkled with salt on a clean kitchen towel.

5. Heat oil in kadhai for deep frying. Add the brinjals. Fry turning sides on medium heat till they change colour and turn brownish. Check with a knife and remove from oil when they turn soft.

6. For gravy, heat 2 tbsp oil and add onion seeds and mustard seeds. Wait for ½ minute till they crackle, add boiled onion paste. Fry till onions turn light golden. Do not make them brown.

7. Add the freshly ground peanut-sesame paste & fry for 1-2 minutes. Add ½ cup water. Boil.

8. Add strained tamarind juice. Mix. Add fried baingan. Boil and simmer for 2-3 minutes on low heat. Add cream. Check salt. Remove from fire. Serve hot.

SIMPLY DELICIOUS

BROWN
CURRIES

Kashmiri Dum Aloo

Serves 4-5

INGREDIENTS

400 gms (8-9) small size potatoes - peeled
1 tsp red chilli powder
2 onions - sliced
4 tbsp oil
4 cloves (*laung*)
1" cinnamon (*dalchini*)
1 bay leaf (*tej patta*)
a pinch asafoetida (*hing*)
2 tsp *degi mirch* powder
1 tsp dry ginger powder (*sonth*)
2 tsp fennel powder (*saunf*)
1 tsp salt
seeds of 1 black cardamom (*elaichi*) - crushed
oil for frying

1. Peel and then prick the potatoes with a fork all over.

2. To boil potatoes, put them in a pressure cooker with 1 tsp red chilli powder, 1 tsp salt and about 3 cups water. Pressure cook to give 1 whistle. Remove from heat and put under running water to release pressure. Cool the potatoes.

3. Heat oil and deep fry potatoes all together, to a rich golden brown colour.

4. In the same oil, fry the sliced onions to a rich golden brown colour. Remove from oil. Grind them with a little water to get fried onion psate.

5. Heat 4 tbsp oil. Add cloves, bay leaf and cinnamon. Fry for 1 minute.

6. Add asafoetida. Add fried onion paste and degi mirch powder. Fry for ½ minute. Add 2½ cups water.

7. Add all other ingredients and the fried potatoes.

8. Cover and simmer till very little gravy remains and oil floats on top.

9. Break one potato and see. The inside should not be white. The colour of the chillies should have penetrated to the centre of the potatoes. If the potato is white from inside add a little more water and simmer for some more time.

10. Serve hot with boiled rice.

Soya Chunks with Capsicum

Serves 4

INGREDIENTS

2 cups soya chunks (nuggets)
1 tbsp lemon juice
1 capsicum or ½ red and ½ green capsicum -
cut into 1" pieces
5 tbsp oil, 1 bay leaf (*tej patta*)
1" stick cinnamon (*dalchini*)
2 brown cardamoms (*moti elaichi*)
1 tsp salt, ½ tsp red chilli powder
2 tsp coriander (*dhania*) powder
¼ tsp turmeric (*haldi*) powder
1 tsp garam masala
½ cup thick curd - well beaten
2 tomatoes - pureed in a blender

GRIND TOGETHER

3 onions - roughly chopped
1 tbsp chopped ginger, 6-8 flakes garlic -
chopped, 2 cloves (*laung*) - crushed

1. Boil 4 cups water with 1 tsp salt and 1 tbsp lemon juice. Add soya nuggets to boiling water. Boil for 2 minutes. Remove from water and let them be in hot water for 5 minutes. Strain.

2. Saute capsicums in 1 tbsp oil in a non stick pan for 2 minutes. Remove from pan. Add 1 tbsp oil and saute boiled nuggets also for 2 minutes. Keep aside.

3. Heat 3 tbsp oil in a heavy bottomed kadhai. Add 1 bay leaf, cinnamon and cardamoms. Wait for a few seconds. Add onion paste. Stir fry on medium heat till golden brown.

4. Reduce heat. Add red chilli powder, coriander powder, turmeric and garam masala. Add curd gradually, 1 tbsp at a time, stirring constantly till dry.

5. Add the freshly pureed tomatoes. Cook for 5 minutes or till oil separates.

6. Add nuggets and stir for 2 minutes to blend. Add 2½ cups of watetr. Give 1-2 boils. Cover and cook on low heat for 2-3minutes. Add capsicum. Bring to a boil. Mix and serve.

Chettinad Curry

Serves 4-6

1 potato - cut into ½" pieces & fried till golden
8-10 small pieces of cauliflower
¼ cup peas - boiled
8 french beans - cut into ¾" pieces
1 carrot - diced into pieces
1 tbsp poppy seeds (*khus khus*)
2 tbsp cashewnuts (*kaju*), 4 tbsp oil
2 onions - finely chopped
3 tomatoes - chopped, 10-12 curry patta
1 tsp salt, or to taste
½ tsp turmeric powder (*haldi*)
½ tsp chilli powder
1 tsp chopped ginger, 8-10 flakes garlic
1 tsp lemon juice, to taste

CHETTINAD MASALA

½ cup freshly grated coconut (remove brown
skin before grating)
1 tsp coriander seeds (*saboot dhania*)
1 tsp fennel seeds (*saunf*)
½ tsp cumin seeds (*jeera*)
2½ tsp peppercorns (*saboot kali mirch*)
5-6 whole, dry red chillies
3 green cardamoms (*chhoti elaichi*)
2-3 cloves (*laung*)
1" cinnamon stick (*dalchini*)
1 tbsp oil

4. Drain poppy seeds and cashews. Grind together the roasted masala with the drained poppy seeds-cashewnuts, ginger and garlic in a mixer grinder to a very smooth paste with ¼ cup water. Keep aside.

5. Grind tomatoes in a mixer to a smooth puree. Keep aside.

6. Heat oil in a kadhai and add the chopped onions. Fry till light brown.

7. Add the pureed tomatoes, salt, turmeric and chilli powder. Cook till tomatoes are well blended with the masala and oil separates.

8. Add the ground paste and curry leaves. Saute for 2 minutes. Add the vegetables and cook for 2 minutes.

9. Add 2 cups hot water. Cover and cook for 5-7 minutes or till the masala is thick and the vegetable are soft.

10. Add fried potatoes. Boil. Add lemon juice to taste if you like. Serve.

1. Soak poppy seeds and cashewnuts in a little warm water for 10-15 minutes.

2. Boil 2 cups water with 1 tsp salt. Add beans, cauliflower and carrots. Boil for a minute till crisp tender. Remove from water and keep aside.

3. Heat 1 tbsp oil in a pan or tawa. Add coconut, coriander seeds, fennel seeds, cumin, peppercorns, dry red chillies, seeds of green cardamoms, cloves and cinnamon to oil. Stir-fry till fragrant. Remove from fire.

Goan Mushroom Xacutti

Serves 3-4

INGREDIENTS

200 gm mushrooms - each cut into 4 pieces
1 onion - finely chopped
1 onion - sliced
3 tbsp oil
2 tbsp tamarind (*imli*) pulp
a pinch nutmeg (*jaiphal*) - grated
1 tsp salt, or to taste

XACUTI MASALA PASTE

½ cup grated fresh coconut
2 flakes of garlic
¾" stick cinnamon (*dalchini*)
2 cloves (*laung*)
1 dry red chilli
¼ tsp turmeric powder
1 tbsp poppy seeds (*khus khus*)
½ tsp carom seeds (*ajwain*)
¼ tsp cumin seeds (*jeera*)
4 peppercorns (*saboot kali mirch*)
½ tsp fennel seeds (*saunf*)
½ star anise (*phool chakri*)
¾ tbsp coriander seeds (*saboot dhania*)

1. Dry roast all ingredients of the xacuti masala paste together in a pan - coconut, garlic, cinnamon, cloves, whole red chilli, turmeric powder, poppy seeds, carom seed, cumin seeds, pepper corns, fennel seeds, star anise and coriander seeds for 2-3 minutes. Remove and cool.

2. In a pan put 4 tbsp oil and fry the sliced onion till golden brown. Remove from oil. Grind the fried onions along with roasted masala to a paste with ¼ cup water till smooth.

3. In the same pan, add chopped onion and cook till soft.

4. Add mushroom and sauté for 5-6 minutes on medium flame till mushrooms turns light brown.

5. Add ½ cup water and salt. Bring to boil and cook covered for 5 minutes.

6. Add prepared masala paste and about 1 cup water. Bring to boil and cook again for 4-5 minutes on medium flame.

7. Add tamarind pulp and boil again. Add grated nutmeg and mix well. Cook for a minute. Serve hot.

Tiranga Paneer ka Salan

Serves 6

INGREDIENTS

200 gm paneer - cut into triangular pieces
1 green capsicum - cut into triangular pieces
1 red capsicum - cut into triangular pieces
4 tbsp oil
1 tsp mustard seeds (*sarson*)
2 tbsp curry leaves
3 onions - grated
a lemon sized ball of tamarind (*imli*) - soaked
in ½ cup warm water
1½ tsp salt, or to taste
½ tsp turmeric powder (*haldi*)

OTHER INGREDIENTS

¼ cup roasted peanuts
½ tbsp chopped ginger
1 tbsp chopped garlic

DRY ROAST ON A TAWA

1 tbsp sesame seeds (*til*)
2 dry red chillies
1 tbsp coriander seeds (*saboot dhania*)
1 tsp cumin seeds (*jeera*)

1. Mash the soaked tamarind and strain to get pulp. Keep aside.

2. Sprinkle salt, pepper on the paneer. Mix well.

3. Heat 1 tbsp oil in a pan and rotate the pan to oil the bottom of the pan. When oil gets hot, add capsicums to the pan. Saute for 1-2 minutes till brown patches appear. Sprinkle a pinch of salt & mix. Remove from pan & keep aside.

4. Dry roast sesame seeds, coriander seeds, cumin seeds and dry red chilli on a tawa till sesame seeds change colour.

5. Make a paste of roasted ingredients along with peanuts, ginger and garlic with ¼ cup water.

6. Heat oil, add mustard seeds, let it crackle and add curry leaves.

7. Add grated onions. Saute until onion turns light golden brown, stirring continuously. Add turmeric powder and mix well.

8. Add roasted masala paste and stir.

9. Stir in 2 cups of water and bring to a boil. Reduce the heat and cook covered for 5-7 minutes. Add imli pulp and salt to taste.

10. At serving time, add paneer and red and green capsicums. Cook on low heat for 1-2 minutes. Serve.

Vegetable Sticks in Curry

Serves 4

1 big potato, 5-6 french beans
2 carrots, few toothpicks

DRY MASALA
2 tsp coriander seeds (*saboot dhania*)
1½ tsp cumin seeds (*jeera*)
1 tsp red chilli powder
½ tsp turmeric powder (*haldi*)
5-6 cloves (*laung*)
5-8 pepper corn (*saboot kali mirch*)
seeds of 6 brown cardamom (*moti elaichi*)

GRIND TOGETHER
2 onions & ½" piece ginger - chopped

OTHER INGREDIENTS
3- 4 tbsp oil
2 tsp of the above dry masala
2 tomatoes - chopped
water - kept aside of the boiled vegetables
½ tsp shredded ginger, salt to taste
¼ tsp amchoor, ½ tsp garam masala

1. Grind all dry masala ingredients together. Keep aside 2 tsp for the curry.

2. Peel potatoes & cut each into ½" pieces or squares. Deep fry to a golden colour.

3. Cut carrots into ¼" thick rounds. String french beans and cut into ¾" pieces.

4. Boil 2 cups of water with ½ tsp salt. Add beans and carrots. Boil for about 5 minutes or till tender. Strain, reserve the water for the gravy.

5. For curry, heat oil. Add 2 tsp of ground dry masala. Add the onion-ginger paste, cook till light brown and oil separates.

6. Add chopped tomatoes. Cook and mash till oil separates. Add shredded ginger & sufficient water of boiled vegetables to get a thick gravy.

7. Add salt to taste, garam masala & dry mango powder. Simmer for 5-7 minutes.

8. Heat 2 tbsp oil seperately in a pan. Add the 2 tsp reserved ground masala.

9. Immediately add the fried potato, boiled beans and carrot and ¼ tsp salt. Mix well for 2 minutes, so that masala coats the vegetables.

10. On a toothpick, insert a potato piece, then french bean & lastly a piece of carrot. Make many such toothpicks and keep aside in a flat oven proof dish.

11. At serving time heat the prepared toothpicks in a hot oven for 2-3 minutes or microwave for a minute. Pour hot gravy on top. Lift up the sticks so that they show on top. Serve hot.

INTERNATIONAL CONVERSION GUIDE

These are not exact equivalents; they've been rounded-off to make measuring easier.

WEIGHTS & MEASURES

METRIC	IMPERIAL
15 g	½ oz
30 g	1 oz
60 g	2 oz
90 g	3 oz
125 g	4 oz (¼ lb)
155 g	5 oz
185 g	6 oz
220 g	7 oz
250 g	8 oz (½ lb)
280 g	9 oz
315 g	10 oz
345 g	11 oz
375 g	12 oz (¾ lb)
410 g	13 oz
440 g	14 oz
470 g	15 oz
500 g	16 oz (1 lb)
750 g	24 oz (1½ lb)
1 kg	30 oz (2 lb)

LIQUID MEASURES

METRIC	IMPERIAL
30 ml	1 fluid oz
60 ml	2 fluid oz
100 ml	3 fluid oz
125 ml	4 fluid oz
150 ml	5 fluid oz (¼ pint/1 gill)
190 ml	6 fluid oz
250 ml	8 fluid oz
300 ml	10 fluid oz (½ pint)
500 ml	16 fluid oz
600 ml	20 fluid oz (1 pint)
1000 ml	1¾ pints

CUPS & SPOON MEASURES

METRIC	IMPERIAL
1 ml	¼ tsp
2 ml	½ tsp
5 ml	1 tsp
15 ml	1 tbsp
60 ml	¼ cup
125 ml	½ cup
250 ml	1 cup

HELPFUL MEASURES

METRIC	IMPERIAL
3 mm	1/8 in
6 mm	¼ in
1 cm	½ in
2 cm	¾ in
2.5 cm	1 in
5 cm	2 in
6 cm	2½ in
8 cm	3 in
10 cm	4 in
13 cm	5 in
15 cm	6 in
18 cm	7 in
20 cm	8 in
23 cm	9 in
25 cm	10 in
28 cm	11 in
30 cm	12 in (1ft)

HOW TO MEASURE

When using the graduated metric measuring cups, it is important to shake the dry ingredients loosely into the required cup. Do not tap the cup on the table, or pack the ingredients into the cup unless otherwise directed. Level top of cup with a knife. When using graduated metric measuring spoons, level top of spoon with a knife. When measuring liquids in the jug, place jug on a flat surface, check for accuracy at eye level.

OVEN TEMPERATURE

These oven temperatures are only a guide. Always check the manufacturer's manual.

	°C (Celsius)	°F (Fahrenheit)	Gas Mark
Very low	120	250	1
Low	150	300	2
Moderately low	160	325	3
Moderate	180	350	4
Moderately high	190	375	5
High	200	400	6
Very high	230	450	7